# CONSCIOUS PARENTING
## WORKBOOK

# CONSCIOUS PARENTING

## WORKBOOK

A Companion and Study Guide to
*Conscious Parenting* by Lee Lozowick

BHADRA MITCHELL
with
Nancy Lewis, Karuna Fedorschak,
Christine McMaster & Matthew Files

HOHM PRESS
Chino Valley, Arizona

© 2014, Hohm Sahaj Mandir and Bhadra Mitchell

All rights reserved. No part of this book may be reproduced in any manner without written permission from the publisher, except in the case of quotes used in critical articles and reviews.

Cover Design: Zachary Parker, zdpdigitalmedia@gmail.com

Interior Design and Layout: Becky Fulker

Library of Congress Cataloging-in-Publication Data

Lozowick, Lee, 1943-2010.
  Conscious parenting workbook : a companion and study guide to conscious parenting / by Lee Lozowick, Bhadra Mitchell with Nancy Lewis, Karuna Fedorschak, Christine McMaster & Matthew Files.
     pages cm
  Includes bibliographical references and index.
  ISBN 978-1-935387-85-5 (trade pbk. : alk. paper)
 1.  Parenting--Religious aspects.  I. Title.
  BL625.8.L696 2014
  649'.7--dc23
                                2014012501


Hohm Press
P.O. Box 4410
Chino Valley, AZ 86323
800-381-2700
http://www.hohmpress.com


This book was printed in the U.S.A. on recycled, acid-free paper using soy ink.

This workbook is lovingly dedicated to Lee Lozowick. His words of wisdom and uncompromising stand for conscious parenting continue to inspire and inform.

# CONTENTS

| | | |
|---|---|---|
| CHAPTER 1 | The Context for Conscious Parenting | 1 |
| CHAPTER 2 | Good Beginnings: Conscious Conception, Pregnancy, Birth and Nursing | 5 |
| CHAPTER 3 | Enough & Never Enough: Love & Affection, and Attention | 11 |
| CHAPTER 4 | Impressions Upon Innocence | 17 |
| CHAPTER 5 | Just Like Us: Role Models | 23 |
| CHAPTER 6 | Drawing a Line: The Challenge of Responsible Boundaries | 29 |
| CHAPTER 7 | No Excuse!: On Child Abuse | 33 |
| CHAPTER 8 | Speaking the Truth: Language and Honesty | 37 |
| CHAPTER 9 | Education for Life: Life in Continuum, the Context of Education and Home-Schooling | 43 |
| CHAPTER 10 | Child's Play: Emotions, Energy Management and Fighting | 47 |
| CHAPTER 11 | Body and Soul: Food, Health, Sex and God | 51 |
| CHAPTER 12 | Radical Vision for the 21st Century | 59 |
| CHAPTER 13 | Sanctuary and Spaciousness: What Our Teenagers Need | 63 |
| CHAPTER 14 | Spiritual Practice for Parents | 67 |
| SUGGESTED READING | | 73 |
| CONTACT INFORMATION | | 84 |

# INTRODUCTION

Greetings fellow travelers on the path to conscious parenting!

By choosing to parent children, or to serve as a friend, educator or informal mentor, you have taken up an admirable and challenging task. Committing yourself to the care and education of children sets you on a journey that is ripe with enormous opportunities for personal growth, expanded love, joy, self-understanding and compassion. It also introduces you to areas of your own life that may have been unexamined, confronting you with limiting beliefs and issues of your own self-esteem.

This *Workbook* is the companion volume to *Conscious Parenting* by Lee Lozowick (Hohm Press, 2010), and is designed be a useful map and "travel" guide for you on this adventure. *The Conscious Parenting Workbook* (like *Conscious Parenting* itself) aims to assist you in aligning with a big view of the subject—an overall context from which to parent and educate. Years of personal experience, combined with solid foundations shared with many great educators, have made Lee Lozowick's *Conscious Parenting* a pragmatic handbook, much appreciated by his peers and by thousands of parents worldwide. But especially, and perhaps uniquely, his work relies on life-affirming principles culled from his own spiritual understanding along with those from other long-standing spiritual traditions. His work, then, speaks to the ways and means for transforming ordinary family life with children into a primary means of spiritual practice, including the inevitable challenge for work-on-self.

Thanks for joining us in this invaluable commitment on behalf of children everywhere.

## WHO WE ARE

Lee Lozowick (1943–2010) was the devoted "Heart Son" of the beggar saint and "Godchild" of Tiruvannamalai, India, Yogi Ramsuratkumar (1918-2001), and a teacher and spiritual master in the Tantric tradition of the Bauls of Bengal, India. Lee's work with his students and friends for over three decades involved his creed of "kindness, generosity and compassion," applied within the framework of daily life. For Lee, a devoted father of six children, the work of parenting, mentoring and educating children was central to his teaching, and he became an advocate for conscious parenting in all its many forms. From enlightened birth practices, breastfeeding, our use of language with children, the limiting of early exposure to technology and negative influences for youngsters, to the creation of environments of safety and sanctuary for our teenagers, Lee demanded that we look at *everything, including ourselves.* Our work was to recognize that our children would "learn to be whole and healthy human beings by living with whole and healthy human beings."

The editors of this *Workbook* are all long-time students of Lee Lozowick. Some of us are parents, others grandparents, others friends of community families, some are mentors for children. We live in different places, interact with different children, and lead lives of busy involvement in our communities. Beneficially, each of us received Lee's teaching firsthand, both in word and action, observing over many years his skillful means and powerful modeling of how to be with children.

## HOW THIS BOOK CAME ABOUT

The inspiration for creating this *Workbook* followed soon after Lee Lozowick's death in 2010, when many of us realized how much his legacy to humanity included this vital teaching, and that carrying on his work of conscious parenting was both our responsibility and our privilege.

We were not alone in this recognition. Members of other spiritual communities, as well as those exploring different educational models, let us know that Lee's vision and work was unique. Rarely had a spiritual teaching (in modern times or in any era for that matter) placed children and child-raising in such a central position. The idea that one could put children in one "room"—so to speak—while pursuing spiritual practice in another "room" was one more way in which ego-bound and immature adults looked for relief from the consequences of their choices. Lee was willing to confront our choices, and to show us—as his master had instructed him—that *everything was God*, and that attention and diligence was called for in every domain of our lives.

Initially begun as a simple book club idea, the *Workbook* naturally evolved into its present form. Chapters from the book *Conscious Parenting* were divided up among us, and bi-monthly meetings occurred via telephone conferencing to review our editorial efforts. Floundering a bit initially to arrive at a workable format, once agreed upon, we began to synthesize and distill the content. Countless hours were spent individually and together discussing what to include and how to word the information. Not surprisingly, while this project became for each of us a dynamic review of the principles of conscious parenting, it soon evolved into so much more. The opportunity for a type of "group work" magnified our individual efforts, even as it demanded a refining of our communication skills and willingness to get out of our own way. The project was bigger than we were! As we reminded one another of this, we were similarly inspired to follow through.

## HOW TO USE THIS BOOK

This *Conscious Parenting Workbook* can be used in a number of different ways, either individually as a study guide, or with interested others in a book club or parenting support group. In any case, it provides, first of all, an invaluable means to review the book *Conscious Parenting* by Lee Lozowick.

While reading a book is one thing, we all know that what is out of sight is often quickly out of mind. Even if we are touched by the author's words, there is always some "next new" thing to grab our attention. Consequently, we typically file away the data or inspiration gained in our initial reading, never revisiting the material or using it to our benefit.

The *Workbook* that you have in your hands is a means for keeping the principles of *Conscious Parenting* alive and vital for you and others. Even if you extend your study of the book for a few additional weeks, you will have taken a decisive step toward encoding these teachings into your own body-mind. Whether you agree or disagree with the author's views, you will be giving yourself the opportunity to engage stimulating and challenging questions about each topic in a way that enables you to clarify your own views, thus establishing your own commitments more powerfully.

For example: In Chapter 6 of the *Workbook* we read:

> The "bottom line" in setting limits is to keep them "honest, sensible, and explainable." What is your experience in setting limits for your children? Do they meet <u>these</u> criteria? What successes or failures are you encountering? What kind of changes might you want to make?

The answers, articulated either alone, in a journal, or with a group of others, require careful information-distilling and assessment. This kind of ruthless (but compassionate) self-honesty can be enormously beneficial. It can open you up to the realities of your life, your way of parenting, your way of being, which can then be used to determine a new world of inspiration and promises.

Secondly, this *Workbook* offers a simple structural tool—a guidebook—for working *together* with others. Conscious parenting engaged as a personal practice can bring up fear, pride, remorse, emotional sensitivity and all the difficulties involved in any human relationship. It is a great gift to have a group in which to share these issues; a place to go where others are enduring the same things.

Sometimes, however, as you probably know, our parent get-togethers become a forum simply for unloading our discouragements or failures, or asking for specific how-to's from each other. And while both of these functions can be invaluable, they may not fully satisfy a deeper hunger, a deeper intuition that we sense in embryonic form. In our experience, the ability to refer together to the wise counsel of a wise elder (in person or through the medium of a book) is a way is to collectively open our own wisdom-minds and compassion-hearts to what we know but may be too timid to accept; a way to up-level our complaints and discouragements to the domain of spiritual practice; a way to create a bonded group support that relies upon grace and the inspiration of a "higher power," in discerning the truth of any situation.

The book *Conscious Parenting* is such a resource. *The Conscious Parenting Workbook* is the auxiliary tool for applying and extending that wisdom.

Because it invites readers to write their reflections and answer questions, the workbook functions as means to clarify our views. There is great help in this. Further, once engaged, it can serve as a useful reference, an "adviser" to look back to when those next thorny issues and confounding situations in parenting naturally arise.

We hope that our results provide benefit to you, and that your results in applying them are more far-reaching and flexible than any of us has initially conceived.

## WITH GRATITUDE

I am very grateful for the all the efforts expended in the realization of this project. I couldn't have, and wouldn't have, done this alone. The synergy and contributions made from my fellow community members made the final result so much better. Five heads (and hearts and worlds of experience) *are* truly better than one…

It is our deepest wish that this workbook be used to effectively support the communication of the teaching on conscious parenting offered by Lee Lozowick. We are grateful for the benefits and blessings we have seen in our own lives through the practice of this great work.

—Bhadra Mitchell

# CHAPTER 1

# *The Context for Conscious Parenting*

## OVERVIEW

*The responsibility of being with children . . . is literally a responsibility for the future of humankind. What we model for children, how we treat them, how we parent them, is more than important—it is absolutely* vital *to their mental, emotional and physical health and well-being and to that of the earth itself . . . Adults need to become conscious parents . . . educated in how to educate children.* — Lee Lozowick

## POINTS

- Children grow to be responsible whole adults by living with adults who are themselves responsible and whole, and who model healthy ways of being rather than preaching moral principles.

- Parents and other adults have the responsibility to provide the kinds of references for children that allow them to be *who they are* without having crippling projections, expectations, and biased demands thrust upon them.

- Children are not "our" possessions to manipulate or dominate. They come through us, and we are here to care for their well-being and education on their journey to becoming whole, mature human beings.

- "Children provide the future for our race . . . The mood of conscious parenting is one of bringing a certain responsibility for *life itself* to our relationships with children."

- Children are by nature innocent and totally trusting. Parents need to care for them in a way that does not abuse that trust.

- Parenting together with other mature adults who share a similar goal and compatible values can be an invaluable resource in supporting our efforts to parent consciously.

- Conscious parenting is about developing a resonance to what is objectively right or optimal for the upbringing and health of the child. Within that context, "doing the right thing" is not a subjective response but is appropriate to the situation. A mature adult knows and takes responsibility for what is objectively true and acts appropriately and with integrity in serving a child's needs.

- Children touch our hearts deeply and in their innocence can awaken in us compassion for a suffering world. They "naturally and effortlessly keep us present" and grounded in the real world if we let them.

- Constant and tacit love is the basis for relationship with children, set in an appropriate context and "an environment of caring . . . so deep and accepting, and so intelligent in relationship to who our children are essentially and developmentally, that our children know they're loved, without a doubt."

## QUESTIONS

1. What arose for you when you first saw your newborn? How can you use that memory as a tangible reminder for supporting your child's essential self today and as he or she continues to grow?

2. What does it mean to allow children to *be who they are*? How can you facilitate that for them? How do you facilitate that for yourself?

3. What adult in your life held the context of love and acceptance of your essential self when you were a child? In what specific ways did they hold that for you?

4. "Finding and getting together with others who have similar values in child-raising can be an invaluable resource." What opportunities are available to you to access this kind of support? Do you feel the need for it?

5. What agendas and/or expectations are you aware of having for your child and perhaps even for yourself as a parent? How do those agendas and expectations affect your parenting?

6. What is your understanding of what it means to parent from a place of context rather than content?

# NOTES

# NOTES

# CHAPTER 2

# Good Beginnings: Conception, Pregnancy, Birth and Nursing

## I. CONCEPTION

### OVERVIEW

*Conscious conception is when one surrenders their humanness and their personal process to the movement of the Divine. It has nothing to do with deciding that you want this perfect being . . . It has to do with surrender, with submission to what the Universe needs or wants.*
— Lee Lozowick

### POINTS

- The choice is not ours as to whether and when a child is created through us. The consciousness of the being taking incarnation chooses the time and place. It is a magical process.

- Our children do not "belong" to us. Yet although they are not "ours," we are responsible for training and educating them in a way that allows them to grow into mature, whole human beings.

- Most people want or have children for completely selfish and neurotic reasons and consequently cause great suffering for the children.

- A loving, affectionate, accepting, respectful and honoring relationship between the prospective parents is crucial for conscious conception.

- Before, during, and after pregnancy a healthy diet, exercise, right thinking and a right relationship to God is recommended.

## II. INFLUENCES DURING PREGNANCY

### OVERVIEW

*Relax. Keep good company. Enjoy a basic healthy diet. Avoid stressful situations, severe emotional states, and any use of chemicals or drugs that affect the nervous system. When birth control is used, the more natural the method used the better. Hold the upcoming birth with enthusiasm, excitement and gratitude, in mind and in attitude.*

### POINTS

- Communicate to your unborn child from the beginning of conception in a positive, encouraging and healthy way, both psychically and verbally.

- Be aware that the fetus "hears" everything and feels our subtle prejudices. Strive for clarity and ruthless self-honesty about expectations and unconscious needs you may have of/for the child.

- Maintain a mood of kindness, generosity and compassion around you and within you, before and after birth, as this mood gets communicated to the child even before birth.

## III. BIRTH

### OVERVIEW

*Surround yourself with supportive, nurturing people who recognize the mystery and magic of birth. Natural childbirth is recommended "to bring[ing] children into this world in a manner that will dispose them to best fulfill their capacity as human beings." If intervention is needed, it is important that the mother stay as connected as possible to her body and her child and "not abandon the birth project."*

### POINTS

- "The actual conditions of birth directly affect how a person manifests in life, in psychological terms." In order to transcend identification with the body and understand a being's true possibility as a human being, parents must create a space that engenders safety and right relationship to God and Life.

- The best birthing situation is one that is natural, without the use of drugs, with those in attendance alert and welcoming, holding an appropriate context of awe and reverence.

- Create a space for the birth that is simple and welcoming, preferably a room with soft, quiet colors and free of music—a space of communion and celebration. Continue to talk to your baby psychically or verbally during the birth, as you would to an adult.

- After the birth, it is recommended that mother and baby remain in the house together for approximately two weeks before venturing out into more stimulating environments.

- As outside stimuli are introduced, you can objectively describe to your baby what these new noises and lights are, and assure him or her that he or she is safe and need not feel threatened.

- During conception and pregnancy, communication and relationship are key elements. "Always turn children toward the Divine, toward wholeness and a natural relationship to life, toward service to others, toward happiness and self-confidence."

## IV. NURSING

### OVERVIEW

*Nursing (breastfeeding) is a powerful bonding activity, "the beginning of a relationship in which the caregiver respects and responds to the child's expression of her own needs, rather than the adult defining the child's reality for her, dictating what the child should need and how the child should respond."*

## POINTS

- It is recommended that nursing be "on demand" and continue as long as the child is actively nursing and the mother is physically capable, ideally for three to five years.

- There is a vital connection between early feeding experiences and the child's psychological and emotional development.

- As the child grows and the mother senses the time for weaning approaching, she can begin preparing the child by talking about when nursing will end.

## QUESTIONS

1. If you are pregnant, what suggestions/recommendations from this chapter are you considering implementing in order to provide a "good beginning" for your child?

2. If you have already had a baby, what conscious choices have you instinctively made that are suggested in this chapter? Describe your experience as a result of making these choices. What is working and what isn't? What might you consider changing?

3. What support do you have or can you create for yourself in order to put into practice ideas you've encountered in this chapter?

4. What expectations are you aware of having for your child and for yourself as you move into a parenting role? Do they expand or limit your options in creating a healthy environment and relationship with your child?

5. Are there any recommendations in this chapter that you find yourself questioning or that raise a conflict in you? What are they? Can you describe the nature of the conflict or disagreement?

# NOTES

# NOTES

# NOTES

# CHAPTER 3

# Enough & Never Enough: On Love & Affection, and Attention

### OVERVIEW

*There are two basic dispositions that human beings have: feeling loved or unloved. If children feel loved in the first two years of life, then whatever else happens in relationships, the unconscious motivating factor of feeling loved will sustain them. Children who feel loved just as they are naturally feel confident, creative, capable, and possess self-respect. If children feel unloved, their life then becomes a pursuit for love from a place of scarcity and insecurity.*

### POINTS

- At a very early age (probably several months) children are aware that the unconditional love they seek could be denied. When this denial does occur, infants are so traumatized that they shut down to avoid feeling the pain. Children can only love, and consequently they expect love from others.

- Children who feel unloved grow into adults who feel unloved. These adults then attempt to compensate with accumulation of power and possessions to establish security and to fill the void inside.

- Children who are properly loved during the first years of life "are big enough" human beings to be able to assimilate, respond, and adjust to many negative circumstances in their lives.

- The best foundation we can give children is the knowledge that they are loved, wanted and enjoyed.

- "Conditioned love"—in the form of expectations, desires and demands that are foisted on children by parents at an early age—sets up an unhealthy mechanism for achieving love.

- Consistent, trustworthy love, acknowledgement, and genuine respect by peers and mates can assist in transcending the verdict of "unlove," but the actual undoing of it is only accomplished through "rewiring" involving hard work and therapy.

- Parents are encouraged to allow children to express love in their own ways, and to model for them spontaneity and a wide assortment of affectionate behaviors.

- Withdrawing affection based on upset is never an appropriate response by parents.

- If affection shared between parents is not equally shared with their children, the effect can be devastating to the self-esteem of the children, as well as negatively impact their entire matrix of feeling expression.

- The form of our relationship to our children may vary, but the consistency of love never should.

- All children's actions are based on a desire to receive love. Providing acceptance, support, encouragement and acknowledgement in all circumstances is crucial.

- Children need healthy loving male *and* female role models, to balance their own masculine or feminine energies.

- No amount of affection is too much when it arises out of unconditional adoration, and when it asks nothing in return.

- Conscious parents do not use affection as a means of control or bribery, nor do they require children to behave in any particular way to receive authentic affection.

- Setting boundaries is a necessary part of parental love. Children need boundaries "to figure out how human society works."

- Attention and intentional communication are keys to a healthy relationship with children. Responding to them immediately supports the belief that they are valued and that they exist.

- Being relaxed and natural in our attention toward our children equates to being present and responsive from the body versus responding from ideas and "shoulds" of the mind.

- The attitude and mood we bring to any task we are involved in has great impact on our children. No matter what is going on for us, if our children need us, we must then shift our attention and priority to what is necessary for them.

- Spending time helping and being with our children, and not putting anything in front of their needs, unless unavoidable, is a challenging and advanced practice that parents need to undertake.

- Doing what is wanted and needed for our children at any given moment is essential in allowing them to know they are being cared for and loved.

- Grandparents are not the parents of their grandchildren, and accordingly should not be providing strong parental boundaries and education.

## QUESTIONS

1. Did you feel unconditionally loved as a child? If so, how was that communicated to you by your parents?

2. What are some expectations that were imposed on you as a child? How has this affected your relationships with your spouse and children/child? How would you like to be in those relationships?

3. How do you show love and acceptance to your child?

4. What ways were you "conditioned" to behave in your early years? What "conditioning" have you observed in yourself as a parent that seems to go against parenting consciously? How are you dealing with this?

5. On page 72 (in Revised Edition), the author summarizes the section "Children First—The Highest Life Practice" by saying: "Put the child first, that's real practice . . . seeing what's needed and wanted in the moment and fulfilling it is a very high practice, always." What is your response to this "high" calling to practice parenting in such a way? Have you experimented with this, and, if so, what is your experience thus far?

# NOTES

# NOTES

# NOTES

# CHAPTER 4

# *Impressions Upon Innocence*

**OVERVIEW**

*Children's true innocence should be maintained as long as possible to foster an inner strength that is flexible and sustaining. Innocence maintained until six or seven years of age will foster young adults who have access to purity, integrity, compassion and kindness.*

**POINTS**

- Innocence is not the same thing as naiveté. True innocence needs an equal vision of both the glory and misery of life to blossom and flower.

- Children are naturally wide open and accepting of whatever they see, without discrimination. It is therefore best to expose them to a broad spectrum of life that is nonviolent in nature and informed by music, art, and different types of people and cultures.

- First impressions are often the most lasting for children, as they are impressions without discrimination. They are templates that become a guide for how life is, which is carried into adulthood.

- When interacting with children, mature adults are conscious of the content and manner in which communications are made. The content should be clean, unprejudiced and free of conditioned falsehoods.

- Providing appropriate, life-positive "impression foods" is a big part of raising confident, happy children and maintaining children's innocence. Mature discrimination is called for in a parent's selection of such "foods."

- "What children see, hear and sense, and what they learn from what they see, hear and sense, can dramatically affect their connection to all aspects of life."

- The longer that parents can leave children to learn and develop within the limits of their organic nature without sophisticated mechanical "help" like TV and computers, the longer their innocence will last and the greater the depth and breadth of their understanding and imagination.

- Choosing toys for our children that are made from organic materials and that foster creativity is healthier for their growth and education than "a mountain of mass-produced plastic toys."

- Being judicious in the timing and quantity of toys dispensed is an equally important consideration in conscious parenting.

- Choosing playmates for our children who have their innocence intact and are kind, generous and life-positive is far more important than choosing playmates with parallel lifestyles.

- Vigilance is needed to allow children to grow naturally into an ability to be both discriminating about and appreciative of a wide variety of experiences and types of people.

- Choice of clothing and shoes is an important consideration in conscious parenting. Going barefoot outside, when possible, in appropriate weather and situations, is healthy for children and allows them to connect with the earth and its subtle energies.

- Children have a natural delight in their bodies. Allowing them to go naked in a non-shaming environment, when appropriate, helps them develop a healthy attitude toward their bodies.

- Travel is a fantastic way to expose children to different cultures and experiences and affords them new and wonderful impression foods. When discordant elements are present, simple and honest explanations assist in making the experience a growth opportunity.

- Other adults can be of great benefit to the development of a child by being "enlightened witnesses" of who children are . . . witnesses of their "inherent innocence and self-worth."

- Unconscious behavior in parents that is acted out in front of children can be traumatizing. If parents are able to honestly relate to and work with their own underworlds, their courage will have a very positive effect on their children.

- Modeling a "no problem" attitude, that life *is what it is*, and that we are ultimately in the hands of God, allows children to gain the ability to make distinctions and have discrimination about their lives that will enhance their health and well-being.

- Children need an environment of health, gentleness, respect and clarity. They need parents who can contextually recognize and honestly communicate when dissonance is present.

- When taking children into an unknown environment, forewarning them of what will be going on prevents them from internalizing new experiences from a place of fear and apprehension. Children need to be assured when in new environments that they are safe and cared for.

- Communication is essential for children when they encounter dissonance in the world. The goal is not to shield our children from the suffering of the world, but rather to explain to them what is going on from a perspective that allows them to understand.

- Children naturally suffer in two specific ways. One is the reality of suffering that occurs from organic incarnation. The other occurs as a reaction to violence, abuse, war, pain, confusion, etc. Parents are encouraged to not buffer their children against the latter kind of suffering as such buffering often enforces an unconscious mechanism of denial.

- Children who have their innocence intact are not afraid of seeing death. Parents need to monitor their own fears and denials around death and not impose them on the children. Instead, parents are to encourage their children to understand that life is a continuum and that one form moves into another endlessly.

- Children have the ability to live in many different realities at the same time. Parents should not deny, limit, or label these other realities in any way, negative or positive.

- Creating projections of any kind about a child's appearance or emotions or behavior can be damaging to their development into their own essential self.

- Children who are encouraged to investigate and follow the urges of their imaginations and curiosities, and to make their own explorations have a greater potential to grow into their essential selves.

- Continuity in existence is important to children. They have a real need to know of their history to establish proof of their existence in this dimension. This is fostered by children hearing stories about their infancy from parents and friends.

- Despite the need for history, often provided through mementos and photographs, children are encouraged to be fully present to their lives on a moment to moment basis, instead of through a collection of sentimental subjective possessions.

- The goal of conscious parenting is to allow children to grow up naturally.

- Assigning age appropriate responsibilities to children provides for some level of learning around responsibilities, while not fostering the need for them to grow up before their time.

## QUESTIONS

1. What does the term "impression foods" mean to you? What types of impression foods do you remember as a child? What impression foods do you want to offer or have you already offered to your children?

2. Are you aware of any "psychic influences" in your own life as a child or as an adult? Are you aware of any psychic influences your child might be dealing with now?

3. What does it mean to "define" our children? How were you defined as a child? How did you step out of that definition and move towards your true self? How can what you've experienced in this domain serve you in parenting consciously?

4. What are some tangible ways in which you can foster imagination, curiosity and exploration in your children? Who in your childhood did that for you, and in what ways did it manifest?

5. How can parents "allow children to grow up naturally?"

# NOTES

# NOTES

# NOTES

# CHAPTER 5

# *Just Like Us: Role Models*

## OVERVIEW

*Children want to be like us. If parents are appropriate role models, children will naturally follow suit. "A child instinctively knows right human behavior from twisted or aberrated human behavior. If the child's role models are living rightly, the child will follow their behavior and grow up sane—psychologically strong and personally balanced." If the role models are neurotic, psychotic, or depraved, that behavior will also be copied, resulting in great pain and suffering for the children from an unconscious crisis in knowing what is instinctively right, compared to how they are living and behaving.*

## POINTS

- All children look for and will choose role models.

- To some degree parents unconsciously choose their children's role models through the environments and influences they expose them to, like movies, TV and video games.

- Children want to be like their parents and will model themselves according to parental actions rather than words. If parents are living rightly and treat their children with love, attention and consideration, the children will grow up sane, balanced and happy, and as adults will choose people to be in relationship with who are likewise.

- The primary responsibility of parents to children is to treat them with respect, be responsible and reliable. "Everything else will take care of itself."

- Children instinctively know objective truth. When they "lose their innocence" by having trusted individuals act contrary to what they know to be true, they develop defense mechanisms to protect themselves against the dissonance between what they know and what they see.

- Parents don't have to be perfect role models. Children can handle occasional bursts of negativity as long as parents are self-honest and don't blame the children for their (the parents') problems.

- Children are fiercely loyal to both parents, and experience conflict if either is attacked by the other. Therefore, it's best if parents do not argue in front of them, especially if criticism of the other parent is involved.

- Children need to see parents' vulnerability and humanness. It's okay for parents to be sad or embarrassed, or to cry in front of the children.

- Children are naturally compassionate and have an innate sense of integrity. When parents model compassionate humanity, this then allows children to witness and practice it.

- Parents should not expect to see immediate results of lessons and values learned by children from role modeling. Parents need to have faith in the good examples they've provided, and in their children's inherent goodness and integrity.

- It's important for parents to let children develop their own opinions rather than superimposing adult opinions on them, even when the parents/adults think their views are refined and compassionate.

- A child's primal imprint on mother is that she is God. A female child instinctually feels the God imprint and the heavy responsibility for service that it represents.

- A male child instinctually knows he is not God, and wants to be. Training boys to be God is a patriarchal reaction when they instinctively know they are not God. This in turn causes internal conflict, with its corresponding "pain, violence, abuse and blindness."

- In today's high-tech, indulgent world, much of the instinctive mothering response has been buried, and mothers are busy with their own lives while children are left to find their role models in TV cartoon characters and superheroes.

- The mother's role is to *be there* for her children, not just physically but with full attention, even at the expense of personal time and preferences.

- Uncompromising self-honesty will reveal the instinctive knowledge that will guide the mother in caring appropriately for her children.

- Little boys need "soft, accepting, loving nurturance" from their mothers, along with appropriate boundaries. "Smothering" rather than mothering often produces the tendency for boys to be more aggressive than girls.

- Bonding with both the mother (the feminine force) and the father (the masculine force) is essential for balance in a children's development. Children should have attention from both parents from birth on, and ideally fathers should be available to children as close to fifty percent of the time as possible. Both men and women should be kind, generous and loving, not too soft and not too tough with their children.

- A willingness to take feedback from other parents about parenting, especially for first-time parents, is essential.

## QUESTIONS

1. "What is required to be Mother is an almost zealously singular attention on the child . . . It is my recommendation that for two years a mother basically has no life of her own, but belongs to her child." What is your reaction to the author's radical call for this level of sacrifice? How do you see it in reference to the

challenges you are encountering or anticipate encountering in your own parenting?

2. Aside from you and your spouse, who or what are the most significant role models in your children's life? What behaviors and qualities do you see them modeling? Which of these behaviors and qualities do you feel are positive and which are negative? What actions might you take to change the ratio?

3. Do you solicit and get feedback about your parenting from other people? Who are they? How do you evaluate the feedback? Do you tend to be open to it or defensive? If you don't have a source of feedback, where might you find it? Are you comfortable giving feedback to other parents when it is requested or when you feel you have something of value to offer?

4. The author recommends that fathers be available to their children as close to fifty percent of the time as possible. How do you interpret this recommendation? How does it work in your family?

# NOTES

# NOTES

# NOTES

# CHAPTER 6

# *Drawing a Line: The Challenge of Responsible Boundaries*

## OVERVIEW

*Parents' basic responsibility, beyond being role models for children, is to be reliable with discipline, the setting of firm just boundaries. "Children need to learn the definitions, limits and extents of their world and* the *world." Children raised without reliable consistent boundaries grow up confused, unsure of themselves and their behavior, and often act out negatively in an attempt to have boundaries placed on them.*

## POINTS

- Children want and need boundaries. Being a conscious parent requires defining limits that make sense and can be simply explained in language they can understand.

- The major teaching about boundaries gets communicated to children between the ages of four and six. If they're not getting the boundaries they need at this time, they will communicate it by acting out in negative ways.

- Consequences for violating boundaries should be immediate, fair, non-arbitrary and appropriate to the situation.

- Generally, the less boundaries the better. The primary boundary is related to physical health and safety. Secondary boundaries are dependent upon circumstances/situations and the age of the children.

- Children will question parents about the boundaries they set and their discipline choices. Children do this to learn about their world and not necessarily to challenge the parents or defy authority. It's not personal.

- Children need to learn that different people do things differently, and the boundaries of a space outside the home may differ from those inside the home. They should be taught to be responsive to the authority of whatever space they are in, as in visiting other children's homes, where the "responsible adult" is in charge.

- Whenever possible, parents should agree beforehand on boundaries and discipline, and not counter one another when children attempt to polarize them to get what they want. The goal is to maintain consistency and unity.

- Children need parents to be trustworthy, reliable and good for their word. If parents are not reliable and consistent, they may permanently lose credibility.

- Parents should allow children to experience being in spaces where certain protocols are observed, and be ready to leave the space when it's apparent that the children need to be in a less structured or formal environment, regardless of parental preference to stay in the space.

## QUESTIONS

1. "Responsibility means recognizing in any given circumstance what is required, and surrendering our own uptight preference in order to do what is required by the larger circumstance. And that is a principle that holds across all boundaries." What do you interpret this statement to mean? What does it bring up for you? How might you work with it both personally and as a parent?

2. The "the bottom line" in setting limits is to keep them "honest, sensible, and explainable." What is your experience in setting limits for your children? Do they meet these criteria? What successes or failures are you encountering? What kind of changes might you want to make?

3. It is the parents' responsibility to help their children learn "objective discrimination" relative to appropriate behavior in spaces—formal or informal—rather than to teach them "manners" that are rigidly applied. What is your experience in dealing with your children in public spaces? How invested are you in your children "looking good"? How might you loosen the hold that investment has on you? What kinds of support might you need to do that?

# NOTES

# NOTES

# CHAPTER 7

# *No Excuse!: On Child Abuse*

## OVERVIEW

*Child abuse, in both blatant and subtle forms (physical and psychological), pervades our culture. The only truly effective way to address the problem is to begin "at home" by doing the work necessary to face our own childhood experience of abuse and thus avoid making the same mistakes with our own children.*

## POINTS

- We must honestly deal with our unexamined psychological labyrinth (programming), if we wish to parent consciously.

- Child abuse is rampant in our culture and is generally unacknowledged in its more subtle forms.

- The written work of psychologist Alice Miller is recommended study material particularly for her emphasis on subtle expressions of violence and disrespect of children.

- An immature parent may treat his or her child as a showpiece to be dominated and manipulated at the parent's whim.

- If we are not part of the solution, we are part of the problem. It is necessary to actively work against child abuse in ourselves and thus begin to dismantle its rampant expression in the world.

- Unless we really see our own expressions of abuse toward children, we are destined to perpetuate the cycle.

- The most thorough and ruthless self-examination is called for to get at the roots of child abuse.

- In innocence, an abused child will usually assume they somehow "deserve" the treatment they receive.

- Children love their parents no matter how they are treated by them. Children invest their parents with a powerful and abiding love and trust.

- Children will selectively remember the "good stuff" from their growing up and thus invent a happy childhood and a loving family whether this was the case or not.

- To buffer ourselves from the abuse experienced in childhood, we shut down the full spectrum of feelings—good and bad—so as to lessen the intensity of the pain.

- We don't need to hide strong or intense feelings from our children, but we must never make them the objects of our anger and frustration.

- It is never acceptable to mistreat a child because you have a conflict with his or her parent.

- Abuse in childhood affects the rest of a person's life because he or she is left with a primal impression of being unloved.

- In our public institutions, we have taken the fear of sexual abuse of children too far. Good teachers and childcare providers have been wrongly accused of abuse for showing natural affection to children. In this scenario, it's the children who lose out.

- Inappropriate behavior toward children from another adult, if handled sensitively by parents, can have negligible impact.

- Children must be protected from an abusive home environment. Sometimes this means that the protective parent will have to take the child and leave the situation.

- It is not necessary or possible for parents to redress all wrongs and failings with their children. If parents truly come to terms with their own childhood abuse, their children are automatically released from its effect on them.

- To continually focus on past personal issues is a waste of time, energy and resources. Attending to the present—with all its potential and possibility—is much more beneficial. Put personal history in the past. That's where it belongs.

## QUESTIONS

1. What are your most vivid childhood memories? Could there be more to your picture of the past than you typically recall?

2. What was your view of the author's definition of "abusive"?

3. Do you think you were abused as a child? If so, how?

4. How do you deal with feelings of anger and frustration when they arise with your child? Are such feelings problematic, or workable, for you?

5. It's not easy to face unpleasant or ugly aspects of ourselves in our dealings with our children. Would you be willing to share something you've seen about your capacity to be abusive with children?

# NOTES

# NOTES

# CHAPTER 8

## Speaking the Truth: Language and Honesty

**OVERVIEW**

*Parents' use of language will literally shape the worldview and self-definition of their children. In conscious parenting, parents aim to nurture and guide with a light touch, allowing children to be who they truly are, free of undue suffering/constraint. To this end, it is particularly important to self-observe regarding the effect of parents' words on children.*

**POINTS**

- Speak respectfully to and about children.

- Avoid baby talk. Use adult language. Children will understand the sense of parents' words, even in utero.

- Avoid laying expectations and preconceived ideas on children.

- Do not threaten children in anger. Parents must always be bigger than their anger, especially with children.

- Don't talk about children in their presence as if they weren't there. Even if they are sleeping, children do hear and will have a reaction/response to what is said.

- Never criticize children's parents when children are present.

- Don't draw negative attention to children's natural body smells and sounds.

- When parents make a boundary with their children, their tone of voice and attitude contribute to the communication as much as the words they use. A natural, non-condescending approach serves best.

- Children can be shamed into compliance, but from this approach parents will affect behavior modification not real learning or understanding in their children.

- Don't use demeaning or humorous nicknames for a child.

- Make positive suggestions to children instead of negative commands.

- Speak to children in age-appropriate and respectful terms, i.e., don't talk about dating or "hot chicks" to a nine year old.

- Inappropriate use of language, as with physical abuse, leads to the loss of innocence in children. Unconscious remarks from adults teach children to be false and manipulative.

- Be sure to immediately and clearly (but discreetly) counter the unconscious remarks of strangers to children in the grocery store or other public places.

- It's not necessary to be bland in speech to children, just truthful, real. For example, saying "I'm starving" when we're hungry is a lie, but "I'm really hungry and so ready to eat!" is alive and honest.

- Avoid the word "sick" to describe minor illness (like a cold) because it teaches an unhealthy orientation to the body.

- Avoid labeling children as "mean" based on their behavior. Rather, hold their basic goodness and determine what they need to be different.

- In general, call children by their names. There is a place for genuine terms of endearment but take care in this regard not to demean or belittle children, or to be overly sentimental toward them.

- Don't talk down to children, but also use language and concepts they can understand, as in saying a road trip will be "three hundred miles," which children will generally not be able to grasp, versus saying it will be "three hours" or a "long time."

- When children are learning to talk we don't need to correct their every mispronunciation, but rather trust their learning process to provide correction over the long haul.

- Regarding compliments to children, be natural or real rather than either effusive or dismissive.

- It's not necessary or possible to be perfect with children, just acknowledge mistakes as soon as you recover perspective.

- Showing children our authentic emotional reaction to their behavior (as in breaking down in tears when we have been pushed to our limit), can be a powerful lesson to children about their effect on the world around them.

- Be truthful about the nature of reality with children, i.e., "If you whack a delicate toy against the wall, it will probably break." If they decide to do it anyway, allow the reality to sink in without being compelled to fix it for them.

- Allow children their grand ideas of what they can do. Who are we to limit or judge what is possible for them?

- Make time for children, and show real enthusiasm to be with them.

- Parents need to be good for their word with children. Children learn reliability in this domain from them.

- Parents shouldn't make promises they can't or won't keep. It's often best to be non-committal with children about future plans rather than disappoint them with arrangements that don't/won't happen.

- Be on time.

- Parents must be honest with themselves about the full range of feelings that arise with their children. It's not all sweetness and light. It's the failure to face the difficult emotions that is the problem, not the emotions themselves. If parents are realistic in this way, they are actually less likely to "lose it" as often with their kids.

- One popular educational seminar program used to introduce the subject of children in this way: "You have to admit that children are a royal pain in the ass sometimes." People dislike this statement because they are in denial about their negative feelings about child-raising.

- One of the causes of child abuse on the part of "devoted" parents is this: "We try to love our children all the time, no matter what." When parents fail to do so, they experience a crisis of self-hatred for imagining they don't love their children, which then produces explosive violence at the perceived source of the problem—their children.

## QUESTIONS

1. There are many suggestions for the appropriate use of language in this chapter, which would seem to imply there is much refinement possible in this domain. Do you generally relate to the points in the text or not? Why do you relate, or not relate?

2. Do you have a childhood memory of a situation that illustrates the impact of language either negatively or positively? How did you feel then?

3. How do you think you measure up as a parent with the use of language? Can you think of a situation with your child that demonstrates the impact of language either negatively or positively?

4. How do you handle the situation when you have made a mistake with your child? Are you satisfied with your current approach and why?

# NOTES

# NOTES

# NOTES

# CHAPTER 9

# *Education for Life: Life in Continuum*

**OVERVIEW**

*Integrating children into "life as it is," in the adult day-to-day world within the culture they're born into, develops self-confidence and self-trust. Such a child is prepared for learning* how *to learn and for developing discrimination* about *what* to learn.

**POINTS**

- Make children full-fledged members of the culture even before birth by establishing a mood of celebration and joy regarding the anticipated birth.

- Allow children from an early age to witness all the things parents do in their daily lives.

- It is recommended that children be kept "on" or in close contact with a parent's body as much as possible until two-to-three years of age, as the parent goes about normal daily activities.

- Allow children to help out with daily tasks appropriate to their age and ability.

- Children take what we call "play" seriously. It is their work.

- Forcing children to help out around the house is usually counterproductive.

- The more parents play and work with their children, the more deeply and easefully children integrate into their parents' world.

- Children respond to the expectations parents hold for them even when unspoken.

- The context of parents' expectations is far more important than the content.

- Children can quite easily learn in a nonlinear fashion, and don't always need to be paying attention the way parents think they should be to learn something.

- Most modern education is unbalanced and feeds only the intellect. A balanced education includes acknowledging and feeding the feeling dimension as well.

- To really relate with children, adults need to be able to "feel into" who the children *actually are* at any given age, instead of focusing on who adults *think children are*.

- Support children's passions as much as possible with defined yet flexible boundaries.

- Effective home-schooling requires fully integrating children into the life of the home, including its inhabitants and routines, rather than solely focusing on a school curriculum.

- Parents must be aware of their own parents' failings in raising them if they want to have any hope of not continuing the same failings in raising their own children.

## QUESTIONS

1. Do you believe it is possible to integrate your children into your adult world?

2. Do you try to include them in your ordinary daily activities? What difficulties do you come up against in attempting to do that?

3. What expectations do you hold for your child? Do you see those expectations as being in his/her best interest?

4. In what ways do you feed your child's passions? Were your parents able to feed your passions as a child?

5. "Without a relationship to children's needs and states of mind, there is no way to effectively teach them." What does this statement mean to you and how do you feel about it?

# NOTES

# NOTES

# CHAPTER 10

# *Child's Play*

## OVERVIEW

*Children learn a great deal from the examples of the adults in their environment. Parents need to allow for a wide range of emotional and basic energetic expressions, especially the ones they find dissonant or annoying. All of the activities of young children are in the context of play, even the ones where difficulties may arise. Parents need to learn to trust that most difficulties their children have with other children can be worked out fine on their own.*

## POINTS

- Allow children a full range of emotional expression.

- Children can learn that it is their choice to be happy.

- Screaming and flailing are normal in children who aren't having their needs met.

- In response to tantrums, hold children close and tell them they are loved.

- Parents need to understand the nature of energetic polarities, and that a child's wide swings of energy are often just his/her attempts to bring balance.

- Allow children to learn the results (tears, upsets, arguments) of their unmanaged energy.

- Even at a young age, children understand when parents talk to them about energy management.

- Children manage well together without parents having to monitor their every interaction.

- Parents can hold an expectation for their children to be kind, generous and compassionate; yet parents must also hold that if their children are not being that way, this too is okay.

- Children naturally establish a "pecking order" with friends and siblings. This practice (and all the inherent inequalities) are normal and do not require adults to intervene to make everything all right.

- Parents' abilities as adults to work out issues with each other will be directly modeled by their children.

- Children work out difficulties both internally and with others in their own way.

## QUESTIONS

1. How well do you deal with high levels of energy in children? Do you find it problematical?

2. How do you handle high-volume noise in children's play?

3. Do you find it necessary to monitor your children's play with others? If so, why?

4. Is it difficult for you to allow your children to work out their own stuff?

5. What do you find that your children are learning from your personal energy management?

6. Do you view yourself as a good role model for working out difficulties with others?

# NOTES

# NOTES

# CHAPTER 11

# Body and Soul: Food, Health, Sex and God

## I. FOOD

### OVERVIEW

*The key to a child's healthy relationship to food, as in all areas, is our non-judgmental and sane perspective . . . you don't need to be too righteous or dogmatic, but just eat basically healthy, live food, and don't worry about it having to be perfect . . . Just use common sense, get as clean food as you can, and relax.* — Lee Lozowick

### POINTS

- If children are not psychologically biased toward food by the righteous or prejudiced attitudes of the parents, and if healthy foods are available, their bodies will instinctively lead them to choose and enjoy these foods.

- If parents don't like certain foods or if they have strong or rigid food preferences, they should work to not impose them on their children. Let children make up their own minds.

- Allow children to eat what they want, even if they consistently want the same thing for a long time, or if they overeat something that is not healthy. Healthily raised children aren't self-abusive and will learn from experience what their bodies need and can tolerate.

- Don't expect that children's food likes and dislikes will remain the same. Allow them space to change.

- Offer children a variety of natural, fresh, healthy foods and let them eat what and how much they want. Don't set limits that are arbitrary or engage in "nutritional hysteria" when they ask for foods that parents regard as unhealthy. Feed them properly and include lots of treats to supplement a basically healthy diet.

- It's helpful to vary children's diets a bit, both to avoid an exclusive and rigid diet pattern, and to allow their bodies to recognize and be able to handle a variety of food substances, including sugar. Travel is an opportunity to experience cultural food differences and specialties.

- If children's dietary habits at home are sound, even if they change in young adulthood when they're on their own, they will likely eventually revert to early, healthier habits.

- Don't cripple children by teaching them to equate food with love by using it as a reward for "good behavior" or by substituting it for physical affection or emotional connection. Don't deny them food as a form of punishment.

- Healthy snacks for children are important as fuel for growth and are fine, providing they don't interfere with participation in meals and are not used to counter boredom.

- Mealtime behavior should be appropriate to the age of the child and to the protocol of spaces.

- Children don't automatically need to be fed first. Integrate them into the timing of meal service in a way that is natural and appropriate.

- Children should be encouraged to participate in mealtime cleanup activities as are age appropriate and not be taught to expect others to do for them what they can do for themselves.

- Allow children to discover and observe their unique eating style without allowing food and eating to become a means of mischievous behavior.

## QUESTIONS

1. What are some of the primary issues around food that you're dealing with in relation to your children?

2. What is your personal relationship to food? How do you see it impacting your children's relationship to food?

3. "Food is a more primal domain than sex, so to be unhealthy in relation to eating, to ingestion, to the nurturance that food is, is a basic dis-ease that can easily affect all areas of adult life negatively." What is your personal experience relative to this statement?

4. What arises for you in response to the author's recommendation to let children eat what they want? If you practice this in your home, what is your experience with it?

## II. HEALTH

### OVERVIEW

*If we live a healthy life, our children will learn that from us as they observe us and practice our lifestyle over time . . . It is our job to care for our children, and if our principles of living are genuine and true, our children will learn them.*
— Lee Lozowick

### POINTS

- Avoid "smother-mothering" children by overindulging health concerns. This behavior runs the risk of training them to be sick and compromising their natural innocence.

- When children have minor scrapes and bruises, treat the symptom directly and appropriately without unnecessary drama.

- Children are amazingly resilient and recover quickly.

- Being overly attentive and indulgent when children are sick encourages sickness as a way to get attention and may promote a pattern of hypochondria in later life.

- Parents should not teach their children to be whiners, nor should they expect children to "tough it out" and be little heroes. This form of parental behavior is child abuse.

- Parents should not allow their own biases and beliefs about health to prevent them from seeking appropriate medical attention and treatment for their children when it's called for. Denying this medical attention or treatment is also a form of child abuse.

- Children's primary aim in life is to be exactly like their parents. If the parents' life and health practices have integrity, that's what the children will learn.

### QUESTIONS

1. How do you see your personal relationship to health being reflected in your children? How do they handle being sick or injured? How do you handle it?

2. The author labels those with rigid beliefs about health and health practices "health purists." Would you describe yourself as a "health purist"? If so, what impact does this have in relation to your care of your children when they are sick or injured?

3. Do your life and health practices have integrity? What does that mean to you, and do you see room for improvement? Where and how?

# III. SEX

## OVERVIEW

*Whether sex and sexuality . . . are overall healthy, or overall unhealthy and twisted, depends on our body-image, and with the feelings associated with bodily pleasure (and our love of pleasing others) or the suppression of or disgust with bodily functions and feelings. All of these impressions are taught us very early in life . . .* — Lee Lozowick

## POINTS

- Whether parents' personal conditioning regarding sex and love was healthy or not, they can instill in their children a healthy, natural relationship to their own sexual being.

- In general, children's sexual programming will develop in accordance with the relationship to sex and the body modeled by their parents and by other adults in their environment.

- Repressive sexual attitudes, not permissive values, will increasingly breed aberrant behavior.

- Parents should neither hide their bodies from nor unnecessarily expose them to their children, but assume an unaffected naturalness in regard to them.

- Playing with their genitals is a natural behavior for both male and female children and should be treated as such. Letting children follow their own instinctive inclinations will result in the development of a "natural social etiquette" in relationship to such play.

- Making love with a mate in a bed or room shared with young children is natural while the children are asleep. Regularly talking with children about the noises or movement they might experience occurring during adult lovemaking will help the children to be relaxed and comfortable.

- Children who are raised consciously in a loving, supportive environment fully express and share their enthusiasm and their curiosity with others.

## QUESTIONS

1. Are you comfortable with your own body and sexuality? How do you see your level of comfort influencing your ways of relating to your children in this area?

2. What is the policy regarding nakedness in your home and family? Did it arise organically or is it an issue that creates conflict or discomfort? How are you dealing with it?

3. What are your feelings about genital self-play in children? How do you address this issue in your home? Do you agree that a child will instinctually develop a "natural social etiquette" about masturbation?

4. Is there any particular issue dealt with in this section that you're particularly uncomfortable with? How might you deal with that?

# IV. GOD

## OVERVIEW

*Talking to our children about God, if we believe in such a thing, should be natural . . . just a matter of using the right language . . . what a child can understand . . . For children to live a life of spiritual practice, or holistic beliefs and lifestyle, they need to see adults who are living this way.* — Lee Lozowick

## POINTS

- Formal religious instruction should not be given to children before puberty, which is a time of consciousness expansion and growing independence.

- Children should be allowed to perceive what they naturally perceive at whatever developmental level they are at, and have their questions answered without being fed data that is beyond their ability to comprehend or integrate.

- Storytelling is a healthy and effective way to stimulate the imagination and allow a gradual integration of higher truths with young children.

- Children will live a life of spiritual practice and relationship to the Divine consistent with what they see the parents living and practicing.

- Children can be trusted to make up their own minds about God and spirituality without being subject to indoctrination into a specific religion or ideology.

- Children are basically innocent and basically good. When allowed to develop their own opinions and sensitivities, they will see and naturally respond to the injustices of the world.

- Don't make a distinction between the sacred and the ordinary to children.

## QUESTIONS

1. What spiritual values do you want to model for your children?

2. Do you agree with the author that children can be trusted to come to God—or not—in their own way without being indoctrinated into or influenced by your own ideology? How are you handling "the religious question" with your children?

3. Do you agree that children are basically innocent and good and will naturally respond to the injustices of the world? Do you see evidence of this in your own children?

# NOTES

# NOTES

# NOTES

# CHAPTER 12

# Radical Vision in the 21ˢᵗ Century

**OVERVIEW**

*Children raised consciously, as we're addressing here, are extremely bright and smart . . . Any child with that kind of bright intelligence can make his or her way in the world if they have radical vision, and we have to give our children this radical vision . . . If we role model a type of radical vision for our kids, they'll go out and experiment with all aspects of life, as all young people do, but they will return to the core values we've represented . . . If we are willing to stand for what we've committed our lives to, our kids might spit and kick, but they will come back, they will want such a committed life for themselves.*

— Lee Lozowick

**POINTS**

- When children are raised with respect and intimacy they will always return to the values of their family.

- All that is necessary is that children have strong role models whose priorities and commitments are in place.

- Home-schooling is highly recommended where children are not encouraged to conform to some success norm, as usually happens in conventional schooling.

- By making a radical decision for children's education, they can adapt to anything, i.e., alternative schools, home-schooling.

- Children's education and adjustments to life are influenced by the attitudes they receive about things.

- The author invites us to consider:

- "Life is basically good."

- "The body can heal itself."

- "We can trust God."

- How might these attitudes, if integrated in yourself, create or affect the circumstances of your life?

- How parents were trained to view security is not meaningful today. Most radical ideas that result in money-making projects are not based on education, but come from an innate genius.

- Parents need to make sacrifices with their time, schedule and lifestyle in order to match their commitment.

- "If we are working our asses off to get our kids an education like we had or like we still believe in, we are passing our agreement in 'success' as a social norm along to our children."

- Children naturally have passions and talents they want to pursue. Parents can support them in this with radical vision and commitment, not necessarily by conventional standards.

- Parents need to train their children to manage crisis, by managing it themselves in their own lives. This does not mean educating children about how corrupt the world is, but rather by being able to sustain commitments and not get swept away by emotional responses.

## QUESTIONS

1. What values were you raised with? How have they changed as you have grown up? What values about life have you imparted to your children?

2. What is your view of success for yourself and your children?

3. What attitudes about life have you consciously or unconsciously modeled for your children?

4. How have you supported your children in following their interests?

5. How well do you manage crisis? How well do your children manage crisis?

# NOTES

# NOTES

# CHAPTER 13

# Sanctuary and Spaciousness: What Our Teenagers Need

## OVERVIEW

*Home, as a sanctuary characterized by a mood of nonjudgmental spaciousness, is a place where our children can breathe fully, relax and know they are loved unconditionally, just because they are our children.*

## POINTS

- Parents are potentially the strongest role models for teenagers and should therefore demonstrate what it is to be a "wise elder."

- A teenager's show of rebelliousness and acting out is not a true indicator of his or her inner states.

- A teen's innocence may get masked by the need to fit in with his or her peers.

- Parents should never lie to their children, but be honest in a way that is sensitive and understanding.

- The fact that teenagers act out and rebel doesn't mean they will always be that way.

- True spaciousness, which is distinct from neglect, is one of the healthiest educational moods parents can hold for children.

- Children will come to their own conclusions about what is actually best for them if parents give them the space to do that.

- If parents' lives are sane, healthy and wholesome, it is likely that their children will choose to live sane, healthy and wholesome lives as well.

- Teens are naturally experimental, and if they are raised intelligently and with respect and affection they will usually return to a sane and healthy life.

- The home needs to be a sanctuary where a teen knows it's always safe to go, under any circumstances, without being subject to shaming or criticism.

- As children get older, parents need to make more and more exceptions to the boundaries set for them.

- It is not a parent's job to make sure children maximize their potential in school and in life, no matter what personal preferences or agendas a parent may have for them.

- Parents must allow children the ability to make their own mistakes and learn from their own experiences.

- Parents need to trust that if their children's essential nature is not repressed, their intrinsic nobility and dignity and basic goodness will guide them in their lives.

- For children to respect parental guidance, they need to feel safe and secure from violence and sermons.

- Self-confidence and happiness are the signs that children have been raised in a home that is their sanctuary.

## QUESTIONS

1. "As a parent you should have one primary aim, relative to your children: that your home is sanctuary for those children." How successful do you feel you are at providing sanctuary for your children?

2. In what ways might you improve or strengthen the mood of sanctuary and spaciousness in your home?

3. In what areas do you feel you have the most difficulty in remaining nonjudgmental about your teen's behavior: choice of friends, attitude toward school, leisure activities, etc.? Where might you look for help in negotiating these areas?

4. Do you recall that your home was a sanctuary for you when you were a teen? In what ways do you identify with your own teenager in the problems he or she is dealing with?

5. Do you find that your children respect you? If not, how do you handle it?

6. Are you able to connect with your children's innocence even in the midst of their rebellion?

# NOTES

# NOTES

# CHAPTER 14

# Spiritual Practice for Parents

**OVERVIEW**

This chapter is specifically directed to spiritual practitioners of any tradition. It promotes the point that conscious parenting is both a measure of and training in basic human maturity.

> *Parenting is a practice which, if truly engaged, is more consuming than that of a Zen monk sitting zazen during a sesshin. It lasts not three days or a month, but almost twenty years, day and night, without interruption. It is also a practice that, once begun, cannot be dismissed or forgotten . . . This is a practice that, once accepted, carries its own built-in momentum that requires our ever-deepening attention, vulnerability, service, sacrifice and surrender.* — Lee Lozowick

**POINTS**

- The job of parenting is long term and fully consuming, and has the potential to be a very thorough spiritual practice.

- Just "becoming *human*" is a worthwhile aim; a place to begin from in making a real difference in our lives and the lives of those around us.

- Parents do love their children, but often don't know how to express that love in a way that communicates it to their children.

- Being human produces a foundation of strength, clarity, dignity and nobility that ultimately enhances our ability to connect with the Divine.

- Parents' neurotic psychologies prevent them from becoming fully human, yet to manage their "unmanageable psychology" may be nearly an impossible task.

- Parents might as well strive for the impossible (managing their psychology, becoming human, attaining enlightenment) because it *has* been done. Some of the greatest realizers were just regular folks to start with.

- If the energy of the Universe begins to flow into our system, every weakness in that system will be exposed. If parents want universal energy to express itself through them as service and compassion, not hatred and greed, they must become human.

- If parents are spiritual practitioners, they can't help but relate appropriately to children.

- Children are an instant feedback mechanism about a parent's genuine maturity in and understanding of the truth.

- Women typically shoulder much of the burden and sacrifice of child-raising.

- Being a parent usually entails a sacrifice of some outer forms of practice (like participation in group meditations or services). However, parents are given the opportunity to learn to practice *internally* within the primary relationship to their children.

- Raising children can be as worthy and valuable a sadhana (spiritual practice) as one that appears more important on the surface of things.

- It is suggested for parents that formal practice be secondary to proper care and attention to their children.

- It *is* healthy and valuable for children to see parents engaged in formal practices like prayer or meditation, but by being fully with them in their growing-up years, parents model the very context that is at the heart of any real practice.

- Parents don't need to give up subtle practices like kindness and patience, but just apply them in parenting.

- Parents, especially mothers, are responsible for nurturing children, who will either help alleviate the suffering of God or add to the suffering of God; who will either serve or obstruct the process of life.

- Raising children often creates a profound attachment that causes them to "lose" a relationship to the truth of non-duality. Parents can reclaim that wisdom by relinquishing "ownership" of their children, allowing them to be who they are as human beings.

- On the other hand, mimicking non-attachment to children is a denial and rejection of relationship with them, and a cruel shock to their innocent assumption of relationship to parents.

- The author favors allowing children access to many adult spaces and sacred spaces. This then puts parents in the position of having to sense the protocol of such spaces, and having to assess the real needs of the children, to decide what will work for them. This can be a demanding practice, but one that is more beneficial than having rigid rules for children.

- Following the "no rigid rules" practice with children in public places may draw critical attention from others. Parents need to be particularly patient and skillful to navigate such situations.

- Conscious care of children is a commitment that extends to all adults who spend time with children.

- When parents make the choice to embrace the raising of children as spiritual practice, they let go of other ambitions, if only for a time, and sacrifice attachments that put themselves first. What they get in return is invaluable: a reconnection to their own unencumbered innocence and the pure joy of truly human love and relationship.

- Having children and being a parent is not necessary to complete one's life or spiritual development.

- Despite the play of appearances, Reality is completely neutral. Parents' relationship to the swirl of the phenomena they experience is generally *not* neutral. In truth, life is about freely choosing to accept *what is, as it is, here and now*. This acceptance can change negativity to bliss.

- To make a family an ashram or sanctuary, it is necessary to be open-hearted, service-oriented, and patient. If parents are successful, their families *will* notice.

- "Idiot compassion" is an expression coined by Tibetan teacher and author Chögyam Trungpa Rinpoche, for a kind of blind servitude to others, like children. He called genuine compassion "ruthless compassion." This kind of compassion asks the question "What really serves this person or situation?" even if the answer isn't easy or formulaic.

## QUESTIONS

1. While the concepts in this chapter are valuable to consider whatever your faith, the information is clearly directed to the spiritual practitioner. Do you have a spiritual practice or religious belief that informs your orientation to parenting? If so, would you be willing to say what it is? If you don't have that element in your life, would you like to? Do you know where to begin creating or building that?

2. If you have a spiritual practice, how do you see that practice supporting your parenting? Is your school/path/religion inclusive of parenting practice?

3. If you do formal practices like meditation, how do you manage these with the demands of child-raising? Does your way of balancing these commitments work for you and your children?

4. How have you ever experienced your children as teachers for you?

5. Do you include your children in your daily adult activities (e.g., formal meal spaces at home or out, sacred spaces of prayer and/or worship, cooking, physical work, etc.)? If so, what are your guidelines for integrating them in this way?

# NOTES

# NOTES

# NOTES

# Suggested Reading

Baksh, Nadir, PsyD and Laurie Murphy, PhD. *In the Best Interest of the Child: A Manual for Divorcing Parents.* Prescott, Arizona: Hohm Press, 2007.

Baldwin, Rahima. *You Are Your Child's First Teacher: Encouraging Your Child's Natural Development from Birth to Age Six.* New York: Ten Speed Press/Crown Publishing Group, Third Edition, 2012.

Berends, Polly Berrien. *Whole Child / Whole Parent.* New York: Harper Paperbacks, Fourth Edition, 1997.

Bly, Robert. *The Sibling Society.* New York: Addison-Wesley, 1996.

Bradshaw, John. *Healing The Shame That Binds You.* Florida: HCI Press, 2005.

Brazelton, T. Berry, MD and Stanley Greenspan, MD. *The Irreducible Needs of Children: What Every Child Must Have to Grow, Learn, and Flourish.* Cambridge, Mass.: Da Capo Press, 2000.

Britz-Crecelius, Heidi. *Children at Play: Using Waldorf Principles to Foster Childhood Development.* South Paris, Maine: Park Street Press, 1996.

Caplan, Mariana. *To Touch Is to Live: The Need for Genuine Affection in an Impersonal World.* Prescott, Arizona: Hohm Press, 2002.

Cohen, Lawrence J. *Playful Parenting.* New York: Random House, Ballantine Books, 2001.

Coloroso, Barbara. *Kids are Worth It: Giving Your Child the Gift of Inner Discipline.* New York: William Morrow and Company, 2002.

Elkind, David. *The Power of Play: Learning What Comes Naturally.* Cambridge, Mass.: Da Capo Press, 2007.

_____. *The Hurried Child: Growing Up Too Fast Too Soon.* Cambridge, Mass.: Da Capo Press, 25th Anniversary Edition, 2006.

_____. *Miseducation: Preschoolers at Risk.* New York: Alfred A. Knopf, 1987.

Faber, Adele and Elaine Mazlish. *How to Talk So Kids Will Listen and Listen so Kids Will Talk.* New York: Scribner, 2012.

Fedorschak, Karuna. *Parenting, A Sacred Task: Ten Basics of Conscious Childraising.* Prescott, Arizona: Hohm Press, 2003.

Firestone, Lillian. *The Forgotten Language of Children.* New York: Indications Press, 2008. [About raising children in the Gurdjieff Work.]

Gaskin, Ina May. *Spiritual Midwifery.* Summertown, Tennessee: The Book Publishing Co., Fourth Edition, 2002.

Gerber, Magda and Allison Johnson. *Your Self-Confident Baby: How to Encourage Your Child's Natural Abilities From the Very Start.* New York: John Wiley & Sons, Inc., 1998.

Ginott, Haim. *Between Parent and Child.* NY: Avon Books, 1965. New, revised and updated edition by Dr. Alice Ginott and Dr. H. Wallace Goddard. New York: Three Rivers Press, 2003.

Healy, Jane. *Endangered Minds: Why Our Children Don't Think.* New York: Touchstone, 1990.

Holt, John. *Escape From Childhood: The Needs and Rights of Children.* Wakefield, Mass.: Holt Associates, 1975, 1984. New Edition, Holt GWS, LLC, 2013.

_____. *How Children Learn.* Cambridge, Mass.: Da Capo Press, Revised Edition, 1995.

_____. *How Children Fail.* Cambridge, Mass.: Da Capo Press, Revised Edition, 1995.

_____, and Pat Farenga, *Teach Your Own: The John Holt Book of Homeschooling.* Cambridge, Mass.: Da Capo Press, Revised Edition, 2003.

Kabat-Zinn, Jon and Myla Kabat-Zinn. *Everyday Blessings: The Inner Work of Mindful Parenting.* New York: Hyperion, 1997.

Kitzinger, Sheila. *The Year After Childbirth: Enjoying Your Body, Your Relationships, and Yourself in Your Baby's First Year.* New York: Touchstone/Fireside Publications, 1996.

Kovals, Kathryn J. *Redirecting Children's Behavior: Discipline that Builds Self-Esteem.* Seattle: Parenting Press, 1998.

La Leche League International. *The Womanly Art of Breastfeeding.* New York: Plume, Penguin Books, 1958, 2004.

Leboyer, Frederick. *Birth Without Violence.* Rochester, Vermont: Healing Arts Press, 7th Revised Edition, 2009.

Leonard, Linda Schierse. *The Wounded Woman: Healing the Father-Daughter Relationship.* Boston & London: Shambhala Publications, Inc., 1998.

Liedloff, Jean. *The Continuum Concept: In Search of Happiness Lost.* Cambridge, Mass.: Da Capo Press, 1986.

Louv, Richard. *Last Child in the Woods: Saving Our Children from Nature-Deficit Disorder.* 2005. Chapel Hill, North Carolina: Algonquin, 2006.

Lozowick, Lee. *Conscious Parenting.* Prescott, Arizona: Hohm Press, Revised Edition, 2010.

Mendizza, Michael with Joseph Chilton Pearce. *Magical Parent, Magical Child: The Art of Joyful Parenting.* Berkeley: North Atlantic Books, 2004.

Miller, Alice. *The Drama of the Gifted Child: The Search for the True Self.* New York: Basic Books, 1997. Revised Edition, 2008.

_____. *Thou Shalt Not Be Aware: Society's Betrayal of the Child.* New York: Farrar, Straus and Giroux, 1998.

Miller, Karen Maezen. *Momma Zen: Walking the Crooked Path of Motherhood.* Boston: Shambhala, Trumpeter Books, 2006.

Montagu, Ashley. *Touching: The Human Significance of the Skin.* New York: Harper Collins, 1978.

Neill, A.S. *Summerhill School: A New View of Childhood.* New York: St. Martin's Griffin, Revised Edition, 1995.

Neufeld, Gordon, PhD and Gabor Mate, MD. *Hold On To Your Kids: Why Parents Matter.* Toronto: Alfred A. Knopf, Canada, 2004.

Newman, Jack, MD and Teresa Pitman. *The Ultimate Breastfeeding Book of Answers: The Most Comprehensive Problem-Solving Guide to Breastfeeding from the Foremost Expert in North America, Revised & Updated Edition.* New York: Harmony Books, Random House, 2006.

Pearce, Joseph Chilton. *Magical Child.* New York: Plume, Penguin Books, USA, Revised Edition, 1992.

_____. *Magical Child Matures.* New York: E.P. Dutton, 1985.

_____. *The Biology of Transcendence: A Blueprint of the Human Spirit.* Rochester, Vermont: Park Street Press, 2004, 2002.

_____. *Evolution's End: Claiming the Potential of Our Intelligence.* New York: HarperCollins, 1992.

Pipher, Mary, Ph.D. *Reviving Ophelia: Saving the Selves of Adolescent Girls.* New York: Riverhead Trade Press, 2005.

Placksin, Sally. *Mothering the New Mother: Women's Feelings & Needs After Childbirth—A Support and Resource Guide.* New York: William Morrow and Company, 2000.

Sears, William, MD and Martha Sears, RN. *The Baby Book: Everything You Need to Know About Your Baby From Birth to Age Two.* United Kingdom: Little, Brown and Company, 2003.

Shah, Idries. *Learning How To Learn: Psychology and Spirituality in the Sufi Way.* New York: Penguin, 1981, 1996.

Simkin, Penny and April Bonding and Ann Keppler. *Pregnancy, Childbirth, and the Newborn (4th Edition): The Complete Guide Paperback.* Minnesota: Meadowbrook Press, 2010.

Solter, Aletha J., PhD. *Attachment Play: How to Solve Children's Behavior Problems with Play, Laughter, and Connection.* Goleta, California: Shining Star Press, 2013.

_____. *The Aware Baby.* Goleta, California: Shining Star Press, Revised Edition 2001.

_____. *Tears And Tantrums: What To Do When Babies and Children Cry.* Goleta, California: Shining Star Press, 1998.

Staley, Betty. *Between Form and Function: A Practical Guide to the Teenage Years.* United Kingdom: Hawthorn Press, 2009.

Stettbacher, J. Konrad. *Making Sense of Suffering: The Healing Confrontation with Your Own Past.* New York: Plume, Penguin Books, 1995.

# OTHER TITLES OF INTEREST FROM HOHM PRESS

*CONSCIOUS PARENTING (Revised Edition)*
by Lee Lozowick

The message of this book is that the first two years are the most crucial time in a child's education and development, and children learn to be healthy and "whole" by living with healthy, whole adults. Offers practical guidance and help for anyone who wishes to bring greater consciousness to every aspect of childraising, including: * conception, pregnancy and birth * emotional development * language usage * role modeling: the mother's role, the father's role * the exposure to various influences * establishing workable boundaries * the choices we make on behalf on our children's education . . . and much more.

Paper, $19.95, 360 pages                           ISBN: 978-1-935387-16-9

...

*TO TOUCH IS TO LIVE*
*The Need for Genuine Affection in an Impersonal World*
by Mariana Caplan
Foreword by Ashley Montagu

The vastly impersonal nature of contemporary culture, supported by massive child abuse and neglect, and reinforced by growing techno-fascination are robbing us of our humanity. The author takes issue with the trends of the day that are mostly overlooked as being "progressive" or harmless, showing how these trends are actually undermining genuine affection and love. This uncompromising and inspiring work offers positive solutions for countering the effects of the growing depersonalization of our times.

"An important book that brings to the forefront the fundamentals of a healthy world. We must all touch more." —**Patch Adams, M.D.**

Paper, 272 pages, $19.95                          ISBN: 978-1-890772-24-6

...

*PARENTING, A SACRED TASK*
*10 Basics of Conscious Childraising*
by Karuna Fedorschak

Moving beyond our own self-centered focus and into the realm of generosity and expansive love is the core of spiritual practice. This book can help us to make that move. It highlights 10 basic elements that every parent can use to meet the everyday demands of childraising. Turning that natural duty into a sacred task is what this book is about. Topics include: love, attention, boundaries, food, touch, help and humor.

"There is no more rigorous path to spiritual development than that of being a parent. Thank you to Karuna Fedorschak for remind us that parenting is a sacred task." —**Peggy O'Mara,** Editor and Publisher, *Mothering Magazine.*

Paper, 158 pages, $12.95                          ISBN: 978-1-890772-30-7

**To Order: 800-381-2700, or visit our website, www.hohmpress.com**

# OTHER TITLES OF INTEREST FROM HOHM PRESS

### YOU DON'T KNOW ANYTHING...!
*A Manual for Parenting Your Teenagers*
by Nadir Baksh, Psy.D. and Laurie Murphy, R.N., Ph.D.

This book offers immediate and clear help to parents, family members and teachers who are angry, confused, frustrated, sad, or at their wit's end in dealing with their teenagers. Beyond advice for crisis situations, *You Don't Know Anything...!* informs parents of the new stresses their kids today must cope with, and suggests ways to minimize these pressures for both adults and teens. Patience, caring, vigilance, "street smarts," knowledge of the teenage brain—these are among the many skills that parents today need. The book points the way to those skills, and encourages parents and other adults to resume their legitimate roles in teens' lives.

Paper; 188 pages, $12.95                                     ISBN: 978-1-890772-82-6

• • •

### 8 STRATEGIES FOR SUCCESSFUL STEP-PARENTING
by Nadir Baksh, Psy.D. and Laurie Elizabeth Murphy, R.N., Ph.D.

No matter who you are, and how much experience you've had with kids, becoming a step-parent, sometimes called the "blending of families," is difficult work. The book presents 8 Strategies in the form of action steps to maximize anyone's chances of success in this challenging endeavor. The authors are a married couple, and partners in their own blended family. They have also worked with hundreds of clients over twenty-five years in their counseling practices. "Being responsible for the day-to-day physical, emotional and spiritual care of someone else's children takes a lot of guts," they assert, it takes "persistence, optimism, focus, and love for your new partner, enough to commit yourself to his or her children."

Paper, 188 pages, $14.95                                     ISBN: 978-1-935387-08-4

• • •

### THE ACTIVE CREATIVE CHILD
*Parenting in Perpetual Motion*
by Stephanie Vlahov

Active/creative children are often misunderstood by the medical community, by schools, and by their own parents. Their energy is astounding; their inquisitiveness is boundless. Channeling that energy is not only helpful, but necessary. Supporting that inquisitiveness is essential! This book provides specific hints for coping, for establishing realistic boundaries, and for avoiding labels and easy judgments where any child is concerned. Written in a simple, journalistic style, the author draws from her experience with her two active/creative sons, and those of others, to present a handbook of encouragement and genuine help.

Paper, 105 pages, $9.95                                      ISBN: 978-1-890772-47-5

**To Order: 800-381-2700, or visit our website, www.hohmpress.com**

# OTHER TITLES OF INTEREST FROM HOHM PRESS

*FREE RANGE LEARNING*
*How Homeschooling Changes Everything*
by Laura Weldon

Presents eye-opening data about the meaning and importance of natural learning. This data—from neurologists, child development specialists, anthropologists, educators, historians and business innovators—turns many current assumptions about school-based education upside down. The book's factual approach is balanced by quotes and stories from over 100 homeschoolers from the U.S., Canada, Germany, Australia, Ireland, New Zealand, Mexico, India and Singapore. *Free Range Learning* will also encourage and excite those who want their children to have the benefits, but who are timid to approach homeschooling. This is the only book anyone needs to make the choice and start the process of homeschooling children, and is applicable for young people from pre-school through high school.

**P**aper, 312 pages, 50 b&w photos, $24.95                     **ISBN**: 978-1-935387-09-1

...

*WHEN SONS AND DAUGHTERS CHOOSE ALTERNATIVE LIFESTYLES*
by Mariana Caplan

A guidebook for families in building workable relationships based on trust and mutual respect, despite the fears and concerns brought on by differences in lifestyle. Practical advice on what to do when sons and daughters (brothers, sisters, grandchildren . . . ) join communes, go to gurus, follow rock bands around the country, marry outside their race or within their own gender, or embrace a religious belief that is alien to that of parents and family.

"Recommended for all public libraries."—*Library Journal.*

Paper, 264 pages, $14.95                                         ISBN: 978-0-934252-69-0

...

*THE JUMP INTO LIFE: Moving Beyond Fear*
by Arnaud Desjardins
Foreword by Richard Moss, M.D.

"Say *Yes* to life," the author continually invites in this welcome guidebook to the spiritual path. For anyone who has ever felt oppressed by the life-negative seriousness of religion, this book is a timely antidote. In language that translates the complex to the obvious, Desjardins applies his simple teaching of happiness and gratitude to a broad range of weighty topics, including sexuality and intimate relationships, structuring an inner life, the relief of suffering, and overcoming fear.

Paper, 216 pages, $12.95                                         ISBN: 978-0-934252-42-3

**To Order: 800-381-2700, or visit our website, www.hohmpress.com**

# OTHER TITLES OF INTEREST FROM HOHM PRESS/KALINDI PRESS

*DIVINE DUALITY*
**The Power of Reconciliation between Women and Men**
by William Keepin, Ph.D., with Cynthia Brix, M.Div. and Molly Dwyer, Ph.D.

This book demonstrates a revolutionary type of healing work between men and women, known as "gender reconciliation." Based on 15+ years of development, this process has created remarkable results within groups as diverse as nuns and priests in the Catholic Church, and most recently with members of the South African Parliament. By setting a context of forgiveness and mutual appreciation of the sacredness of life, the women and men of a group or institution are empowered to jointly confront the realities of gender oppression and conditioning. *Divine Duality* describes what can happen when a transpersonal/spiritual dimension underlies such work.

Paper; 320 pages, $16.95                                                                                     ISBN: 978-1-890772-74-1

• • •

*IN THE BEST INTEREST OF THE CHILD*
**A Manual for Divorcing Parents**
by Nadir Baksh, Psy.D. and Laurie Murphy, R.N., Ph.D.

This book will help parents save their children unnecessary anguish throughout the divorce process. Written by a licensed clinical psychologist, and a nurse and counselor, the authors have a private practice with families and also work as court-appointed evaluators in child-custody disputes. Their advice and direction is eminently practical—detailing what adults can expect from a custody battle; what they will encounter in themselves and in their children (emotionally, physically, mentally) during divorce; advising how parents can make sense out of children's questions; offering guidance in making decisions for themselves and their kids; and explaining the ultimate importance of putting the child's needs first.

Paper, 144 pages, $16.95                                                                                      ISBN: 978-1-890772-73-4

**To Order: 800-381-2700, or visit our website, www.familyhealthseries.com**

# OTHER TITLES OF INTEREST FROM HOHM PRESS

### WE LIKE TO NURSE
by Chia Martin
Illustrated by Shukyo Lin Rainey
*Also Available in Chinese Language Version*

Research has documented that the advantages of breastfeeding far outweigh the disadvantages in the overall health of the child. This unique children's picture book supports that practice, as it honors the mother-child relationship, reminding young children and mothers alike of their deep feelings for the bond created by nursing. Captivating and colorful illustrations present mother animals nursing their young. The text is simple and warmly encouraging.

Paper, 32 pages, $9.95

English ISBN: 978-0-934252-45-4
Span/Engl bi-lingual ISBN: 978-1-890772-94-9

•••

### WE LIKE TO NURSE TOO
by Mary Young
Design by Zachary Parker

This children's picture book focuses attention on our kinship with all mammals, using simple text and delightful full-color illustrations of animal mothers naturally feeding their babies. Children learn about the nursing habits of animals they love from all parts of the world—porpoises, dolphins, sea lions, orca whales and others. This book is the sequel to Hohm Press's highly successful *We Like to Nurse*.

Paper, 32 pages, $9.95

English ISBN: 978-1-890772-98-7
Span/Engl bi-lingual ISBN: 978-1-890772-99-4

•••

### BREASTFEEDING
by Regina Sara Ryan and Deborah Auletta, RN, IBCLC
*Also available in Blue 6th grade easy-reading version*

In a short, easy-to-read format, this book pleads the case for breastfeeding as the healthiest option for both baby and mom. With gorgeous photos and 20 compelling reasons why breastfeeding is best, this book summarizes current research about the disease-protective and nurturing substances that breast milk alone supplies. It also stresses the deep physical-emotional bond that breastfeeding establishes between mother and child.

Paper, 64 pages, $9.95

English ISBN: 978-1-890772-48-2
Spanish ISBN: 978-1-890772-57-4

**To Order: 800-381-2700, or visit our website, www.familyhealthseries.com**

# OTHER TITLES OF INTEREST FROM HOHM PRESS/KALINDI PRESS

**READY TO WEAN**
*The Return of the Dangling Red Earrings*
by Elyse April
Illustrated by Diane Iverson

The transition from nursing to weaning is a rite of passage. It can either be a time full of stress, regret and confusion, or a joyous celebration of growth. *Ready to Wean* is a children's picture book designed to empower both mothers and children in the weaning process. The friendly text reassures and prepares the child, in a confident way, for this new stage of growth, and bolsters mother's confidence that she will continue to grow with her child, beyond this particular form.

Paper, 32 pages, $9.95                English ISBN: 978-1-935387-30-5
                                      Span/Engl bi-lingual ISBN: 978-1-935387-60-2

• • •

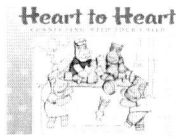

**HEART TO HEART**
*Connecting With Your Child*
by Jeff Goelitz and Elyse April
Illustrated by Laura Stango

This is a book about conscious and conscientious childraising. *Heart to Heart* shares inspirational and practical information to help parents and caregivers of young children lessen their stress and establish healthier communication in their relationships with children. Uniquely designed as a children's book, it encourages adults and children to consider together how they can deepen their bonds of love through care, active listening and genuine attention. Children need the sanctuary and safety that conscious parenting invites.

Paper, 32 pages, $9.95                English ISBN: 978-1-935387-43-5

• • •

**WE LIKE TO EAT WELL**
by Elyse April
Illustrations by Lewis Agrell

This book celebrates healthy food and conscious eating habits. It encourages young children and their caregivers to eat for both energy and strength; and to eat more slowly, frequently, and in smaller amounts. Playful illustrations show children enjoying fresh foods—especially vegetables and fruits—as well as whole grains and "good fats."

Paper, 32 pages, $9.95                English ISBN: 978-1-890772-69-7
                                      Span/Engl bi-lingual ISBN: 978-1-935826-01-9
                                      Spanish ISBN: 978-1-890772-78-9

**To Order: 800-381-2700, or visit our website, www.familyhealthseries.com**

# OTHER TITLES OF INTEREST FROM KALINDI PRESS

### WE LIKE OUR TEETH
by Marcus Allsop

Dental health for children has always been a vital health priority, but now more than ever this issue needs attention.

This bright, whimsical picture book for children and parents will encourage them to care for their teeth. Delightful images show baby and adult animals celebrating their own strong, healthy teeth. The clever, rhyming text offers children and parents the basics of good dental hygiene.

Paper, 32 pages, $9.95

English ISBN: 978-1-935826-06-4
Span/Engl bi-lingual ISBN: 978-1-935826-09-5

• • •

### WE LIKE TO READ
by Elyse April
Illustrated by Angie Thompson

The need for this book has never been greater. *We Like to Read* provides a new look at how to teach and encourage reading by using play and "attachment parenting"—i.e., lots of physical closeness and learning by example.

"I love this beautiful book, filled with the tenderness of all our children's sensibilities and senses. It will be treasured by many, many little ones." —**Jonathan Kozol**, author, educator

Paper, 32 pages, $9.95

English ISBN: 978-1-890772-80-2
Span/Engl bi-lingual ISBN: 978-1-890772-81-9

• • •

### WE LIKE TO PLAY MUSIC
by Kate Parker

Music is the gift of a lifetime and offers an avenue of creative expression for children, individually and together.

*We Like to Play Music* is an easy-to-read picture book full of color photos of children playing music and enjoying music alone or with parents or peers. The rhyming text says how everyone can play music—emphasizing that no special training is needed to shake a rattle, dance to a beat, or even to form your own "band."

Paper, 32 pages, $9.95

English ISBN: 978-1-890772-85-7
Span/Engl bi-lingual ISBN: 978-1-890772-90-1

**To Order: 800-381-2700, or visit our website, www.familyhealthseries.com**

# OTHER TITLES OF INTEREST FROM KALINDI PRESS

### WE LIKE TO HELP COOK
by Marcus Allsop
Illustrated by Diane Iverson

Young children learn by watching and doing. Even toddlers can often help out in the kitchen with simple tasks … sometimes much more than we expect. All the children in this book are helping to prepare healthy foods—parts of the Healthy Diet illustrated by the USDA MyPlate. See www.choosemyplate.gov

Paper, 32 pages, $9.95

English ISBN: 978-1-935826-05-7
Span/Engl bi-lingual ISBN: 978-1-935826-00-2
Spanish ISBN: 978-1-890772-75-8

• • •

### WE LIKE TO MOVE
by Elyse April with Regina Sara Ryan
Illustrated by Diane Iverson

*We Like to Move* is a children's picture book with upbeat, rhyming text and brilliantly-colored illustrations of young children engaging in many forms of physical activity. The book presents multicultural characters—including African-American, Hispanic, Caucasian and Asian children and adults—and varied locales, from a busy city street scene to a country landscape. Each child shown is joyfully demonstrating both the physical and the emotional health benefits of exercise.

Paper, 32 pages, $9.95

English ISBN: 978-1-935826-02-6
Span/Engl bi-lingual ISBN: 978-1-935826-08-8
Spanish ISBN: 978-1-890772-65-9

• • •

### WE LIKE TO LIVE GREEN
by Mary Young
Design by Zachary Parker

This Earth-friendly book provides an introduction to vital environmental themes in ways that will appeal to both young children and adults. We can all recycle and reuse, conserve water or grow a garden! Lively full-color photo montages demonstrate how to make a difference in a world threatened by pollution and ecological imbalance.

Paper, 32 pages, $9.95

English ISBN: 978-1-935387-00-8
Span/Engl Bi-Lingual ISBN: 978-1-935387-01-5

**To Order: 800-381-2700, or visit our website, www.familyhealthseries.com**

# Contact Information

**LEE LOZOWICK (1943-2010), the author of *Conscious Parenting*,** was a father and a dedicated child advocate. As the spiritual teacher for an intentional community based in both the U.S.A. and Europe for over thirty-five years, he worked with hundreds of parents and children in both day-to-day and crisis situations. He is the author of over twenty books, including: *The Alchemy of Love and Sex*, and *Feast or Famine, Working with Mind and Emotions*. Many of his books have been translated into French, German and Spanish. Lee's teaching, known as "the Western Baul tradition," ranges from an emphasis on self-observation and the importance of spiritual practice, to practical direction about family life and human relationships. He was also a poet and lyricist, and the inspiration for a blues band, a rock band, and other musical projects that continue to perform in both the U.S. and Europe.

**BHADRA MITCHELL,** the project manager for this *Workbook*, is a mother, an artist and a former librarian. This project evolved from her deep commitment to the needs of children everywhere.

**ALL THE EDITORS OF THIS *WORKBOOK*** are longtime students of Lee Lozowick. Some are parents, others grandparents, others friends of community families, some are mentors for children. These editors live in different places, interact with different children, and lead lives of busy involvement in a variety of communities. Beneficially, each of them received Lee's teaching firsthand, both in word and action, observing over many years his skillful means and powerful modeling of how to be with children.

# About Hohm Press / Kalindi Press

**HOHM PRESS** (and its affiliate Kalindi Press) is committed to publishing books that provide readers with alternatives to the materialistic values of the current culture, and promote self-awareness, the recognition of interdependence, and compassion. Our subject areas include parenting, religious studies, women's studies, the arts and poetry. We also present the Family and World Health Series, for children and parents, with titles that support nutrition, reading, dental care, environmental issues, and other subjects.

**CONTACT:** c/o Hohm Press / Kalindi Press, PO Box 4410, Chino Valley, Arizona, 86323, USA; 800-381-2700, *hppublisher@cableone.net*

Visit our websites at *www.hohmpress.com* and *www.kalindipress.com*